The Oil of Joy

40 Days of Devotion, Discipline, and Direction

Karen,
May the Joy of the Lord always be your strength.
Thanks for your support !!
N ♡ Joy

Nicole Joy Holmes

It's A Girl! Publishing

The Oil of Joy
Copyright © 2015 by Nicole Joy Holmes

First Printing

Printed in the United States of America

All rights reserved. No part of this publication may be reproduced, distributed, or transmitted in any form or by any means, including photocopying, recording, or other electronic or mechanical methods, without the prior written permission of the publisher, except in the case of brief quotations embodied in printed reviews and certain other noncommercial uses permitted by copyright law.

Request for information should be addressed to:

It's A Girl! Publishing
P.O. Box 1605
Upper Marlboro, MD 20773

ISBN: 978-0-692-43911-1 (soft cover)

All scripture quotations and references, unless otherwise indicated, are taken from the New King James Version. Copyright ® 1982 by Thomas Nelson, Inc. Used by permission. All rights reserved.

Scripture quotations marked (NLT) are taken from the Holy Bible, New Living Translation, copyright © 1996, 2004, 2007 by Tyndale House Foundation. Used by permission of Tyndale House Publishers, Inc., Carol Stream, Illinois 60188. All rights reserved.

Scripture quotations marked "MSG" or "The Message" are taken from The Message. Copyright 1993, 1994, 1995, 1996, 2000, 2001, 2002. Used by permission of NavPress Publishing Group.

Cover Design & Layout: Vincent Multi-Media, LLC
Logo & Back Cover Layout: Hatcher Studios, LLC

This Book Is Dedicated To the Greatest Mom in the World!

Barbara Ann Postell-Jackson

&

In Loving Memory of My Grandmother

Katherine E. Keyes

&

In Loving Memory of Kevin A. Harriday

CONTENTS

Acknowledgements ix

INTRODUCTION xi

Day 1 -   It's Time to Deliver 1

Day 2 -   You Are A Masterpiece! 5

Day 3 -   Don't Worry, Be Happy 9

Day 4 -   At the Cross 13

Day 5 -   The Secret Place 17

Day 6 -   Let Go or Be Dragged 21

Day 7 -   Little by Little 25

Day 8 -   A.N.T.S. 29

Day 9 -   Can You Hear Me Now? 33

Day 10 - All My Children 37

Day 11 - You Are What You Eat 41

Day 12 - Got Friends? 45

Day 13 - Copycat 49

Day 14 - Divine Destination 53

Day 15 - I Feel You 57

Day 16 - What Do You Say? 61

Day 17 - How Much Do You Weigh? 65

Day 18 - Don't Give Up 69

Day 19 - Moving Day 73

Day 20 - Mirror, Mirror 77

Day 21 - The Gift That Keeps On Giving 81

Day 22 - The Place of God 85

Day 23 - The Good Wife 89

Day 24 - Father Knows Best 93

Day 25 - The G.O.A.T 97

Day 26 - Are You Certain? 101

Day 27 - No Laughing Matter 105

Day 28 - Don't Look Back 109

Day 29 - Lemon Pound Cake 113

Day 30 - This Is A Stick Up! 117

Day 31 - This Is Only a Test 121

Day 32 - You Are Forgiven…Kind Of 125

Day 33 - Charge It! 129

Day 34 - Closer Than You Think 133

Day 35 - Membership Has Its Privileges 137

Day 36 - Son-Roof 141

Day 37 - Come Out With Your Hands Up! 145

Day 38 - In God We Trust 149

Day 39 - It's Not For Show 153

Day 40 - Spiritual Withholdings 157

Final Thoughts 161

Topical Index 163

ACKNOWLEDGEMENTS

To Jesus Christ, my Lord and my Savior: I am because You are!

To my beloved husband, Calvin Lee Holmes Jr: You are the most beautiful extension of God's love for me. Thank you for your unwavering love, support, and friendship. I love you eternally!

To my sons, Tyler & Austin Holmes: Sharing in your lives is one of my greatest privileges. I pray that the truth of God's word will always be your compass. I love you both!

To my parents, Barbara & Frank Jackson and Darlene & Calvin Holmes Sr: Thank you for believing in me and for always encouraging me throughout my walk with God. I love you all!

To my siblings, Buster, Alan, Lisa, & Sandy: God has blessed me with the greatest siblings one could ever hope for. I love you all!

To my spiritual mentors: Pastor John K. Jenkins Sr. & First Lady Trina Jenkins (First Baptist Church of Glenarden), Pastor Alan Postell & First Lady Lisa Postell (Greater Destiny Christian Ministries), Pastor Delbert Pope & First Lady Kimberly Pope (Destiny Frederick Ministries), and Bishop Robert Conward &

First Lady Beverly Conward (St. James Restoration Church): Your ministries have forever changed my life for the better. I pray that God will richly pour into you all as you have so tirelessly poured into others!

To Emory Grove United Methodist Church: A house is only as strong as its foundation. Thanks for my foundation!

To Jeffery Rushing, Kimberly McFadden-Johnson, Maria Gomez, and Tynisha Jackson: Thanks for the love, laughs, and loyalty.

To Tawanda Prince & Rey Thomas: Thank you for the trail of bread crumbs you freely left behind for those of us who were lost on the path of self- publishing. God bless you!

To Pastor Donna Scott (Bethel Worship Center): You embody sisterhood! Thank you for the life giving words you spoke over my life in 2010.

Mayor Khidhr: Your incessant optimism is infectious! You have been a constant fixture within my team of supporters. Thank you!

To Dr. Celeste Owens: Your ministry and your testimony has been an inspiration to me. God bless you!

My Heartfelt Thanks To: All of my family & friends who have supported, nurtured, and encouraged me over the years. Your presence and your prayers have been invaluable.

INTRODUCTION

As a young girl, I often felt like a bit of an oddball. I was skinny, awkward, frequently teased about my slanted eyes and my flat chest. I wore my heart on my sleeve and would cry at the drop of a hat. There were also many good times, but the highlight of my week was always Sunday Mornings. Mommy was an early riser and on Sundays she'd faithfully cook us a big breakfast while listening to her "spirituals." I remember the shape of her face, the fold of her lips, and how pretty her smile was and still is to this day. "Hi Mommy" I'd say, approaching the kitchen hoping that she bought Aunt Jemima instead of King Syrup. Even though I would never eat more than one small pancake (or silver dollars as Mom affectionately called my serving). Ever since I can remember I have loved to sing. On the fourth Sunday of each month, I'd scarf down my breakfast so I wouldn't be late for singing in the junior choir.

On my way to church, Mommy watched me as I crossed the street and walked into the little white church on the corner of Emory Grove Road. Before fading from my view she'd say, "Say a prayer for me!"

I vividly remember a particular Communion Sunday when I was twelve years old. I ran in the house after church, changed out of my choir uniform and yelled to my Mom that Mr. Jookie and Miss Minnie said, "Hi." I rushed outside to play, keeping in mind I ate that cracker in church so I had to try not to lie or be bad. Even though I drank the juice too, I still felt awful about the Sour Apple Blow-Pop I stole while at the Seven Eleven the day before. I wondered, "What if I took the 30 cents back to the store, would it still be stealing?" I didn't know what the word repent meant but the guilt ate at me for a long time.

As I grew older, my thirst for knowledge of God grew also. It seemed like the more I sought after Him the more challenges and obstacles came my way. At age 14, one challenge in particular rocked me to my core. I was diagnosed with JRA (Juvenile Rheumatoid Arthritis). As an aspiring Olympic gymnast, that news was devastating to me. My entire life changed in what seemed to be overnight. Physically, I began to feel like a teenager trapped in a 100 year old body. As the disease progressed, I found myself spending more time alone. I reasoned that no one could truly understand how I was feeling mentally or physically, not even God. There were days when I became so depressed I didn't know how I would go on. There were so many things I wanted to accomplish and experience, but this disease appeared to be a threat to all of my possibilities. I came to a point where a decision had to be made. Either I was going to live or I was going to die!

So there I was, standing at the edge of the pool about to end it all. I thought about how in past times I would never do more than insert my toes into a pool as I do when I've drawn a bath that was too hot. I've always had a phobia of large bodies of water, but on this particular day, nothing could keep me from giving up. I was persuaded that this was the most painless way to end it. The alternatives were too horrific. I couldn't stand the sight of my own blood, I had taken enough pills to last me a lifetime, and guns always made me nervous. I had truly reached the end of my rope (no pun intended). What seemed like a lifetime of pain and loneliness would finally be over. This was a decision that I had given careful consideration, and I knew it would have a lasting impact on those I would be leaving behind. But I was confident that there would be peace and rest on the other side.

Once I went in the water, there was no turning back; I would no longer exist. It didn't even matter to me that I couldn't swim. As soon as my body was fully immersed in the water, my whole life flashed before my very eyes. I felt a force while in the water and nothing could separate me from its power. Its current pulled me under like a magnet. Suddenly, a strange yet familiar voice lovingly beckoned me to walk into the light. And I did, willingly. Immediately, all of the hopelessness and despair began to dissipate, and this unexplainable serenity engulfed me. I was beginning to transition to life after death. It was finished...I was dead.

This was the day of my spiritual rebirth, my Baptism. My outward expression of an inward commitment I made to God many years prior. I am grateful for both my trials and triumphs because from each I've learned to praise God. In the words of the late Reverend James Cleveland, "Jesus is the best thing that ever happened to me!"

Throughout the years, I've always felt the hand of God guiding me and keeping me every step of this journey called life. I believe the greatest gift in life is the good news of salvation through Jesus Christ:

"The Spirit of the Lord God is upon Me, because the Lord has anointed Me to preach good tidings to the poor; He has sent Me to heal the brokenhearted, to proclaim liberty to the captives, and the opening of the prison to those who are bound; to proclaim the acceptable year of the Lord, and the day of vengeance of our God; To comfort all who mourn, to console those who mourn in Zion, to give them beauty for ashes, **The Oil of Joy** *for mourning, the garment of praise for the spirit of heaviness; that they may be called trees of righteousness, the planting of the Lord that He may be glorified." (Isaiah 61:1-3 NKJV)*

My earnest prayer for you is that as you reflect upon each devotion within The Oil of Joy, you will be drawn toward a closer walk with Jesus, and as a result will experience the true Joy that Jesus desires we all have.

Day 1
It's Time to Deliver!

I jokingly said to a pregnant colleague, "It seems as though you've been pregnant forever!" She laughed and said, "It feels that way to me too!" Although we both knew from a gestational perspective she would deliver in a matter of days, her 40 week pregnancy seemed a lot longer. In like manner, spiritual births can often seem to take a long time also. Sometimes we spend so much time talking about giving birth to our dreams, goals, and ministries that it may cause others to say to us, "It seems as though you've been pregnant forever!"

When God causes us to conceive (ideas or visions), we don't have to waste time convincing others that we're pregnant. We don't have to wear oversized clothes, walk with a waddle, or wave a wand with pink or blue plus signs. But as with physical gestation, there should be signs of life within our spiritual pregnancy that a birth is about to take place:

Cravings: Your thirst for the things of God increases, and like pickles and ice cream, your appetite for the word of God will appear strange to those who don't understand what God is doing within you.

Growth: Your dreams or goals begin as small seeds implanted by God, but as you work by faith, those seeds begin to develop, grow, and take shape. As you look upon God's spiritual sonogram, you will be able to see the heart of your new business, the eyes of your new ministry, or the legs of earning your degree.

Discomfort: You will become uncomfortable in positions that were once comfortable to you. You will no longer fit in with the old crowd and lifestyles of your past. Sometimes we become content with being pregnant, but there should become a point when our pursuit of progress makes us so uncomfortable, that we have no other choice but to push. With God in the delivery room, our discomfort will become joyful anticipation the moment He says, "It's time to deliver!"

As I labored, pushed, and gave birth to this book, The Oil of Joy, this "baby" prompted me to name my publishing company "It's A Girl!" And by the way… I'm expecting to deliver again any day now and I pray that you are too! ☺

Today's Devotional Reading: Isaiah 26:17-18, Philippians 1:6

Today's Discipline: Monitor the signs of life within your spiritual pregnancy.

Prayer: Lord God, no matter how many things I've started and never finished, no matter how unaccomplished I may feel, with You as my mid-wife I know that I can never miscarry a spiritual pregnancy. I am "confident of this very thing, that He who has begun a good work in me will complete it until the day of Jesus Christ!"

Day 2

You Are a Masterpiece!

When I was in the third grade, my class was given the opportunity to take a piece of clay and mold it into whatever our hearts desired. We were told that these works of art would be given to our parents as gifts. My piece of clay started as a vase, then it became an ashtray, and finally the finished product was a rushed replica of me. I spent so much time molding and re-shaping the clay that the end of class was nearing and I had to make something fast. I quickly squeezed the clay to create a neck and a body, poked two holes for the eyes and one for the nose, made a half-moon smile with my index finger, and I placed it on the tray with all the others waiting to go into the kiln. As my "mini-me" baked in the kiln, the glaze began to crack, and my work of art looked like something you'd need a pooper-scooper to pick up. Nonetheless, with great enthusiasm, I presented my masterpiece to my Mom and beaming with pride she said, "I love it!"

The New Living Translation (NLT) bible says, "For we are God's masterpiece. He has created us anew in Christ Jesus, so we can do the good things He planned for us long ago." Isn't it wonderful to know that ages before you were even born, God already knew everything about you and He still loves you? Before we ever drew our first breath, God already watched every day of our lives like a movie.

Even when we become cracked from the heat of life's challenges, God looks at us beaming with pride and says, "I LOVE YOU...YOU ARE MY MASTERPIECE!" As with all masterpieces, the real beauty is in being able to see the heart of its creator shining through.

Today's Devotional Reading: Ephesians 2:10, Psalm 139

Today's Discipline: Look in a mirror and affirm yourself with the word of God. God cannot lie, so what He says about you is the irrefutable truth!

Prayer: Heavenly Father, I praise You that I am a Designer Original! Help me to not compare myself with the gifts, talents, and uniqueness of others. You crafted me with purpose and You crafted me on purpose. "Marvelous are Your works and that my soul knows very well! "

Day 3
Don't Worry, Be Happy

In 1988, Bobby McFerrin released his hit song "Don't Worry, Be Happy." Even if you tried really hard, it was nearly impossible to not find yourself humming this infectious tune. The first verse is packed with simple but very poignant wisdom, "Here's a little song I wrote, you might want to sing it note for note. Don't worry, be happy. In every life we have some trouble, when you worry you make it double. Don't worry, be happy."

When we worry, our problems tend to appear bigger than they really are. A wise preacher once told me that 80% of the things we worry about never actually happen. That's a huge amount of energy to exhaust on something that probably will never take place.

When I think upon the times when I worried and wondered "what if," most of the time the "what if" never came to pass. And the times when the unthinkable did happen, God had something greater waiting for me on the other side of that change. If we're not careful, worrying can become our first response to every situation.

We must not allow what we see, to change what we know! Jesus was very intentional when He said, "do not worry about your life!" This statement is not a suggestion. God will take care of everything concerning our lives if we let Him.

Today's Devotional Reading: Matthew 6:25-34

Today's Discipline: After reading today's passage of scripture, make a list of all the things you're worried about and use it as a bookmark for Matthew 6:25-34. This symbolizes giving your worries to God. If you decide you want your worries back, you'll have to go to God's word to find them.

Prayer: Dear Lord, Your Word declares that I should "be anxious for nothing." Even when I don't know the way, I know the Way Maker. Strengthen me to trust You with all of the cares of my life and grant me the peace of knowing that true happiness comes from a relationship with You.

Day 4
At the Cross

One of the most joyous occasions in the life of a Christian is the observance of Easter (Resurrection Sunday). Many of us can recall the days of our youth when Easter was a time for egg hunts, baskets filled with plastic grass, jelly beans, and chocolate covered bunnies. The girls were all dolled up in their brand new pastel colored dresses with bows and patent leather shoes; while the boys were decked out in their three piece suits and their snap on ties. Easter was not Easter without the much anticipated television epic, "The Ten Commandments." Who could forget Charlton Heston's classic portrayal of Moses?

As important as these traditions seemed back then, as believers we have come to observe Easter in a far more spiritual and personal way. No longer do we melodiously sing, "Here comes Peter Cottontail, hopping down the bunny trail…" Through spiritual maturity, we understand that Easter is on its way because of the sacrificial Lamb of God!

Jesus died a horrific death for the atonement of our sins. Everything that we are and will become, must be viewed with Jesus and Calvary's cross as a backdrop. Jesus' suffering, sacrifice, life, death, and resurrection should serve as an unwavering reminder of God's love for us. Easter connects us all to eternity and this is truly something to rejoice about!

As we enter this season of reflection and preparation, let us with earnest hearts, seek to discover a deeper intimacy with Jesus Christ, renounce behaviors and habits unbefitting a child of God, and inquire of the Lord His guidance, His wisdom, and His perfect will for our lives. Jesus lives and as a result, we have life in abundance!

Today's Devotional Reading: Isaiah 61:1-11

Today's Discipline: Tithe a tenth of your day (24 minutes) in quiet communion with God.

Prayer: Father God, I thank You that because of Your sacrifice and love for me, I have everlasting life. I could never repay the debt I owe, but by Your grace, I can honor You with a life of service to others. I believe that as I begin to seek Your face, You will reveal to my heart the things I need to surrender unto You.

Day 5
The Secret Place

Growing up, hide and seek was a game that kids could play for hours. Everyone would scurry around looking for a place to hide from the person designated as "it." After a quick count down, "its" job was to locate as many or all of the other children by searching in various places. Think about all of the places you used to hide when you were a kid. For some it may have been behind a tree, bush or car, or if you played hide and seek indoors, you may have hidden in a closet, bathtub, or under a bed. No matter your choice of refuge, the one thing we all had in common was we did not want to be discovered by the person we called "it!"

Ironically, as believers in Jesus Christ, we continue to find ourselves engaged in a daily drill of hide and seek. The only difference is, God is our only true source of refuge and Satan is the designated "it"; "walking about like a roaring lion, seeking whom he may devour." (1 Peter 5:8) Throughout Psalm 91, David encourages us that "He who dwells in the secret place of the Most High shall abide under the shadow of the Almighty." The word shadow can also be defined as shelter and protection. When we hide in the secret place of the Most High, we enter into a level of safety and protection that cannot be penetrated by anything or anyone.

When we find ourselves in trouble and in need of shelter, all we need to do is hide in "The Secret Place" and seek the counsel of the Most High. The best thing about "The Secret Place" is, it's not just a temporary hiding spot, but it's a place where we all can reside. God desires for us to make Him our dwelling place. In good times and in bad, as long as we are "hidden" in Christ, Satan cannot find us.

Today's Devotional Reading: Psalm 91

Today's Discipline: Create a quiet place in your home intentionally used for prayer, study, and worship.

Prayer: Heavenly Father, thank You for being my refuge and my fortress. There is no safer place for me than under Your shadow. You promise Lord, that when I put my trust in You, You will deliver me from the traps of the enemy, be my shield all day long, assign Your angels to be my personal body guard, and satisfy me with long life.

Day 6
Let Go or Be Dragged

I heard a story about an amputee whose expensive prosthetic leg became caught in the door of a departing train. The man frantically attempted to get the attention of the conductor, but the train continued to accelerate. He knew he had one of two choices; either release the lock on his prosthetic leg and let it go or be dragged by the train.

In the fictional albeit symbolic ending of the action movie "Die Hard", starring Bruce Willis (John McClane), terrorist Hans Gruber is falling from a high rise office building to his death. Seconds before he falls, Hans grabs on to the Rolex watch of John's wife Holly, nearly dragging her down with him. In a quick attempt to save his wife, John released the clasp on her watch, and freed her from the weight of Hans pulling her down to certain death.

As in these two harrowing stories, there will be critical times in life, when we will have to demonstrate the courage to let go. In my experience, there are three things we must be willing to let go of to avoid being dragged down. I like to call them the 3P's: People, Possessions, and our Past.

1.) <u>People</u>: We must LET GO of unhealthy, dysfunctional relationships and LET GO of withholding forgiveness from people who have hurt us as a means to punish them, because it really imprisons us.
2.) <u>Possessions</u>: We must LET GO of the material things that we have allowed to become gods or idols in our lives.
3.) <u>Past</u>: We must LET GO of the pains and disappointments of our past that prevent us from living in the present.

Many of us hold on to the 3P's so tightly, that our hands are never free to receive what God truly desires for us to have. Some things require that we free ourselves. We look to God or others to help deliver us from the life sapping baggage that keeps us in bondage, but the plain truth is, NO ONE ELSE CAN FREE YOU WHEN THE CAPTOR IS YOU!

Today's Devotional Reading: Proverbs 6:5

Today's Discipline: Take stock of your 3P's and if you're being dragged, let it go!

Prayer: Heavenly Father, please help me to identify the things in my life that I need to let go. Grant me the wisdom to put nothing or no one before You, the clarity to choose my wholeness over dysfunction, and the strength to always walk in the liberty of being a child of God.

Day 7
Little by Little

Have you ever stood on a promise of God, and you put action with your faith, and nothing happened? Are you waiting on a promise of a new career, relationship, ministry, or a child? You may be trusting in a promise for healing of an illness, a breakthrough in your finances, or a positive change in your marriage, but the evidence of God delivering on His promise cannot be seen.

In today's scripture reading, God makes a promise to the people of Israel to protect them from their enemies, as they travel to the place He had prepared and promised they would possess. Interestingly, with this particular promise, God chose to reveal His timetable at the time the promise was made. God cautioned them that He would not drive their enemies away in one year; rather He would drive them away "little by little." Then God revealed that without their enemies, the condition of the land would be too great for them to handle. God knew they needed time to mature, time to cultivate the land, and they needed enemies to test their strength and faith.

We too need to be prepared for the magnificent things God has in store for us. Think about how a trust fund works. The resources are managed and administered based on the will of the grantor. The beneficiary may receive a lump sum or periodic payments made in small increments over time. The grantor determines how the resources will be disbursed at the time the fund is established, based on their assessment of the beneficiary's level of preparation, maturity, and ability.

God may not reveal His timetable to us. There may be times when God will move quickly on our behalf but sometimes He may move "little by little." We must remember that whether God chooses to fast track a promise or send it by way of pony express, He ALWAYS keeps His promises. Also, we need both time and our enemies to mature and develop us, and there is only one thing that time and our enemies have in common...NEITHER OF THEM ARE ON OUR SIDE!

There are innumerable promises that God will fulfill in our lives. He desires to elevate us to heights unimaginable, but we must not get discouraged when it doesn't happen quickly. So count your blessings and your enemies, and remember that God allows them both to come into our lives;

sometimes all at once and sometimes "little by little." We cannot trust the promise without trusting the process!

Today's Devotional Reading: Exodus 23:23-30

Today's Discipline: Ask God to synchronize your clock to His will!

Prayer: Lord God, even when man defaults on a promise, You always keep Your word. When pitfalls and obstacles are ahead of me, You Lord, are always behind me orchestrating the pace of my steps.

Day 8
A.N.T.S.

In the field of psychology, Automatic Negative Thoughts otherwise known as A.N.T.S., is a common acronym used to describe habitual, dysfunctional thinking. When situations arise that cause us to feel stressed and anxious, A.N.T.S. can come into play. We will find ourselves saying things like "I'm not good enough," "I'll never get married," "Everything makes me look fat," or "How could I be so stupid!" Aside from the fact that persistent self-destructive thoughts can lead to poor self-image, poor health, and depression, our negative thoughts can also lead to negative behaviors. A.N.T.S. can rob us of the joy-filled life God intends for us to have.

Just like the pesky little insects (ants) that try to invade our homes and picnics, A.N.T.S. (Automatic Negative Thoughts) also must be exterminated however, they require a different kind of "RAID." These A.N.T.S require that we **R**UBUKE **A**LL **I**MPURE **D**EDUCTIONS with the word of

God! The bible teaches that we must utilize the tools of God to rid ourselves of all reasoning, thoughts, and logic that are not properly aligned with what God's word says about us. Instead of us saying, "I'm not good enough" say, "I am more than a conqueror through Him who loves me!"

Picture your mind as your home. Would you allow the dirt and impurities from the outside to be tracked all throughout your home? Would you invite a stranger into your home? Consider negative thoughts as strangers who mean us harm, and want to break into our mental homes to rob us of everything! Just because the A.N.T.S. come knocking, it doesn't mean we have to invite them in. Solicitors ring our doorbells all the time, and when we don't answer the door, they leave us alone!

We must practice examining our thoughts. The next time an Automatic Negative Thought comes into your mind, ask yourself, "Would God agree with this thought? Does this thought carry life or does it carry death?" If the answer is "No," use your R.A.I.D. and get your A.N.T.S. under control!

Today's Devotional Reading: 2 Corinthians 10:3-6, Romans 8:37

Today's Discipline: Identify your A.N.T.S. and begin to exterminate!

Prayer: Father, sometimes I am overwhelmed with negative thoughts about my health, my job, my body, and others. Help me to align my thoughts with Your word. Psalm 139:17 says, "Your thoughts of me are precious and numerous." Lord, cause my thoughts of myself and others to be precious also.

Day 9
Can You Hear Me Now?

Several years ago, Verizon Wireless launched a commercial in which one of its employees, who was referred to as "test man," was given the assignment to go into the most obscure places to test the reliability of its network. Test man traveled for miles into mountains, manholes, and swamp lands to ensure that calls could be made and received without interference or the signal dropping. This commercial birthed a catch phrase that was widely repeated by many around the world-"Can you hear me now?"

Although the commercial popularized the catchphrase, it was a phrase those of us with cell phones would find ourselves saying every time we'd lose signal strength while on a call. No matter what cellular carrier you were contracted with, there were certain locations that were simply impossible to get a call through. For me, the most thought provoking part of this advertisement was actor James Earl Jones asking in the background, "How do you build America's largest mobile network? By never being satisfied until that no matter where you go, your call goes through."

Regardless of what circumstance or situation we find ourselves in, we must always make certain that we can connect to God. Not only do we need to be able to connect to God, but we need to be ready and available to answer when God calls us. We cannot allow our trouble spots to cause interference between us and The Lord.

The most important calls we make are to God and with Him there are never any outages, knee-mails (prayers) are always delivered, and we have unlimited anytime minutes. When we find ourselves disconnected from God, make no mistake about which one of us has lost our signal strength!

Today's Devotional Reading: Jeremiah 33:1-2

Today's Discipline: Test your signal strength and re-establish your communication with God.

Prayer: Father God, thank You for always being available when I call You. When I am at my highest or my lowest, let me always create opportunities to connect with You.

Day 10
All My Children

Someone once told me that "God does not have any grandchildren because we are all His children." As Christians, we believe that Jesus is the Son of God and we have received Him as Savior and Lord of our lives. Through our relationship with Jesus, we've come to know His Father (God) as a Provider, a Healer, a Protector, a Comforter, and much more. But how many of us have gotten to know God as our Father? When Jesus prayed at Gethsemane, He cried out to God saying, "Abba, Father!" The term "Abba" is equivalent to the words "Daddy or Papa." It illustrates Jesus' familial relationship to God as His Son. We are _blood_ relatives of God through the death and resurrection of Jesus Christ and God desires for us to know Him as "Daddy" as well.

The Lord's Prayer begins with *"Our Father"* for a reason. *Our Father* wakes us up with a Holy tickle to our bellies that causes a dimpled grin to be our daily countenance. *Our Father* provides us with food when we're hungry and meets all of our earthly needs. *Our Father* gives us His peace during our storms and allows us to jump up into His lap and feel His loving arms nestled around us when we're afraid. When we fall, hurt, or make a mistake, *Our Father* is there to kiss it and make it all better. When our enemies have us cornered, we can shout to them, "I'm *gonna* tell my Daddy!" and *Our Father* will come to our defense. When we are weary, *Our Father* rocks us so closely that we can feel the pulse of His Spirit as soothing as a lullaby. Now that's what I call "Child Support!"

As children of God we are never without a family, we are never without siblings, and we are never without love. We are all His children...check your D.N.A. (Divine Nature Activated)!

Today's Devotion Reading: Mark 14:36, Romans 8:15-17

Today's Discipline: Meditate on today's scripture reading and re-discover "Our Father."

Prayer: Abba, Father, there is nothing in this world that can compare to Your love. My first words may not have been "Da-da" but my heart is overwhelmed that with each day I grow to know You as "Daddy!"

Day 11

You Are What You Eat

Almost every day, health experts feed us the latest information on what to eat and what not to eat. We are advised to eat less sugar and eat more vegetables, scale back on carbs, and increase our protein intake. Dietary studies show that having a balanced diet is necessary to maintain proper health and nutrition. The number of basic food groups varies depending on the source, but they all conclude that when consumed daily they promote growth and optimum development.

Although physical nutrition is vital to our health and wellness, spiritual health is equally as important. The prophet Daniel understood this all too well. Daniel was a strict vegetarian however, his strength and vitality was rounded out through the spiritual sustenance He received from God. Jesus rebuked Satan saying, "It is written, Man cannot live by bread alone, but by every word that proceeds out of the mouth of God."

What we eat spiritually is essential to how we develop spiritually. The bible identifies some food groups that can promote our spiritual growth and development as Christians when consumed daily:

Fish: "...Follow Me, and I will make you fishers of men." (Matthew 4:19)

Bread: "I am the living bread which came down from heaven. If anyone eats of this bread, he will live forever; the bread that I shall give is My flesh, which I shall give for the life of the world." (John 6:51)

Milk: "...as newborn babes, desire the pure milk of the word that you may grow thereby, if indeed you have tasted that the Lord is gracious." (1 Peter 2:2-3)

Honey: "My son, eat honey because it is good, and the honeycomb which is sweet to your taste." (Proverbs 24:13)

Fruit: "But the fruit of the Spirit is love, joy, peace, longsuffering, kindness, goodness, faithfulness, and self-control." (Galatians 5:22-23)

Today's Devotional Reading: Daniel 1:5-17, Psalm 119:103, Matthew 4:19, John 6:51, 1 Peter 2:2-3, Galatians 5:22-23

Today's Discipline: When you start to feel hungry, "taste and see that the Lord is good." (Psalm 34:8)

Prayer: Father God, "You are the strength of my life and my portion forever!" Your word is medicine to my bones and life to my flesh. Help me to have a healthy balance of physical and spiritual nutrition.

Day 12
Got Friends?

"Friends come and friends go, but a true friend sticks by you like family." Proverbs 18:24 ("MSG") One of the most beautiful illustrations of friendship in the bible is the story of Jonathan and David. They were truly B.F.F.'s (Best Friends Forever).

David was literally on the run from a jealous and enraged Saul (who happened to be Jonathan's father). It was prophesied to Saul that because of his disobedience, God had rejected him as king, and David would be his replacement. To add insult to injury, Saul also learned that his son Jonathan made a covenant with David. Saul blamed Jonathan for "stirring up his servant David against him." "Saul sought to kill David every day" and with Saul hot on David's trail, David found himself in the "strongholds in the wilderness." Jonathan risked being perceived as a traitor and jeopardized his relationship with his father to aid David in his time of need. Sometimes our friends will strengthen us by listening to us or comforting us in our times of sorrow. But there is nothing like a friend who will strengthen us in the Lord.

Let's examine what it means to strengthen our friends in the Lord:

1.) Jonathan went to where David was in the wilderness (verse 16). We've got to be willing to meet our friends where they are. Our wilderness places can be dark, lonely, and depressing. Part of friendship involves being willing to go to our friends in their time of need. Jonathan did whatever was necessary to get to David.

2.) Jonathan comforted David with his presence and encouraged him to not fear (verse 17). To have a best friend to talk to or embrace is priceless, especially when we're alone and afraid in our wilderness place. In our modern age of technology, the span of our "cyber friends" are growing daily. We are rapidly moving away from telephone calls and impromptu visits to our friends. We have become so impersonal that texting has become our first form of communication. We should not have to log on to Facebook or Twitter to learn what's happening in the lives of the people nearest and dearest to our hearts. These forms of communication are convenient however there's nothing like getting up close and personal to comfort our friends with our presence.

3.) Jonathan strengthened David in the Lord, by giving David hope through reminding him of God's promises (verse 17). Jonathan reminded David of who he was in the Lord; a king! Ironically, Jonathan being the eldest of Saul's sons was next in line to inherit the responsibility of king. But he recognized God's sovereignty and wisdom, and he graciously accepted David as God's choice. Although David may have grown weary in the process of becoming king, with Jonathan's encouragement, David did not give up on the promise that he would be king. Sometimes we need our friends to remind us of our destiny!

Today's Devotional Reading: 1 Samuel 23:14-18

Today's Discipline: Call or visit a friend, it may be exactly what they need today.

Prayer: Father God, I thank You for the friends that You have placed in my life. Help me to never take them for granted and to always be willing to strengthen and encourage them in You.

Day 13
Copycat

Remember as a kid when we'd do something foolish or reckless, the excuse we'd give our parents was because we saw someone else doing the same thing? Then your Mom or Dad would say, "Well, if they jumped off a bridge, would you jump too!?"

Being a "copycat" seemed to come natural when we were children. Growing up, most everyone I knew loved Michael Jackson & The Jackson 5 and I was no exception. From the cartoon to the albums, to the wall posters, I was a Michael Jackson fanatic. As much as I loved Michael's music, there was a boy in my grade school whose sun rose and set with Michael Jackson. He loved him so much he tried to walk, talk, dance, and dress like Michael. He even glued tiny pieces of aluminum foil to his socks in hopes of achieving "the glitter effect."

As harmless and innocent as his infatuation with Michael Jackson was back then; today our society has moved to a place where imitating unrighteousness and evil has become a common practice. We see adults and sadly some children emulating the vile behavior of characters they see in movies and television or using profane and derogatory language frequently heard in songs on the radio. We see people earn a living preying on the weaknesses of men and women through drugs, alcohol, and prostitution.

It breaks the heart of God to see His children being imitators of evil. Jesus' life on earth is the ultimate illustration of what we should aim to be like. In case you're wondering, being an imitator of God does not mean we have to be perfect. It simply means that we work at becoming fully dependent on Him and that we love Him and others in the same manner that He loves us. When we walk in love and copy how Jesus lived, we develop a beautiful fragrance that God loves to smell and others will want to know where they can get it.

Today's Devotional: Ephesians 5:1-7, 3 John 1:11

Today's Discipline: Ask God for a spiritual makeover so you can be just like Him!

Prayer: Father God, I want to be more like You. Lord, help me to identify and expel any conduct that displeases You. Help me to be an imitator of what is righteous and holy.

Day 14
Divine Destination

Have you ever been lost while traveling and the person driving the car would rather drive around aimlessly than to ask someone familiar with the area for directions? Before the days of GPS (Global Positioning System), we relied on the use of maps or our own sense of navigation to get us to our desired destinations. Back then, there was no talking dashboard companion to provide us with turn by turn directions. Today, many of us have become totally dependent on the assistance of our GPS systems to get us to nearly any geographical location. As technologically savvy as most GPS systems are, there are some instances where they can lead us in the wrong direction and our course is re-routed.

When we lack God's wisdom and we attempt to navigate our own course, without the direction and guidance of God, we will become lost. If God has the map for our lives, how then can we know where we're going without Him? The bible teaches in Proverbs 3:5-6, "Trust in the Lord with all your heart and lean not on your own understanding; in all your ways acknowledge Him, and He shall direct your paths." How awesome it is to know that when we seek God's counsel, He will speak to us and give us turn by turn directions to navigate His charted plan for our lives!

Life's highway can be full of traffic, detours, and potholes but when we travel the path of God, He will make the way smooth and He will position us to reach our Divine Destination. God wants us to rely on His direction for our lives the same as we do the little gadgets in our cars. As with the GPS, God's guidance is also global. No matter how lost we become and how many wrong turns we make, we can ask God for direction, and He will lead us to the right path.

Today's Devotional Reading: Proverbs 3:5-6, Proverbs 20:24

Today's Discipline: God knows where you are and He knows where you need to go. Ask Him to help you find your way.

Prayer: Father God, when I make a wrong turn, usually it's because I chose to go my own way or I listened to ungodly counsel. Help me to always trust You and seek Your wisdom and direction for my life.

Day 15
I Feel You

As I was consoling a friend who was grieving the death of a loved one, another friend walked up and softly whispered to her, "I feel you." In casual vernacular, the phrase "I feel you" simply means "I understand how you feel" or "I sympathize with what you're going through." Although neither of us could personally relate to the circumstances that resulted in the death of her loved one, we both attempted to share in her pain.

When we go through pain, tests, trials, and disappointments, it's comforting to know that those who care about us will offer condolences and encouragement. Sometimes however, our grief is prolonged because we feel no one truly understands our situation. The truth is Jesus really does understand and He can identify with our sorrows and weaknesses. Jesus has seen it all and been through it all and He is well acquainted with our griefs. In fact, He "bore our griefs and carried our sorrows" on the cross, and through it all He never sinned.

When death is God's will, when your friends betray you, when you're challenged with temptation, when you're falsely accused…Jesus "feels you!" The bible declares, "For we do not have a High Priest (Jesus) who cannot sympathize with our weaknesses, but in all points tempted as we are, yet without sin." When we hurt, Jesus hurts. Jesus desires for us to come to Him without hesitation to receive His mercy and grace in our time of need.

Family and friends can be a balm when we're wounded, but there is nothing more healing and comforting than the still, soft whisper of Jesus saying, "I feel you."

Today's Devotional Reading: Hebrews 4:15-16, Isaiah 53:1-6

Today's Discipline: Read today's scripture passages from The Message translation of the bible.

Prayer: Father God, I believe there is nothing I can go through or experience that You cannot understand. Help me to seek Your understanding and empathy when I'm in pain or in trouble.

Day 16
What Do You Say?

All our lives we've been taught that saying, "please" and "thank you" goes a long way. As children, when someone would give us a gift or a compliment, our parents would ask, "What do you say?" and we'd innocently reply, "Thank you." As adults, when someone extends an act of kindness to us, no one should have to prompt us to say "thank you," especially when that someone is Jesus.

Jesus was approached by ten men, all whom were afflicted with leprosy. The men shouted from a distance and pleaded with Jesus to heal them. Bear in mind that because they were considered "unclean," they were deemed social outcasts. Jesus had mercy upon them and commanded them to go to the priest to be declared clean. While they were in route to see the priest, all ten men were healed of leprosy. Of all of the men, only one came back to Jesus, fell to his knees, and thanked Him. Even Jesus asked, "Were there not ten cleansed? But where are the other nine?"

In desperation, these men came to Jesus with a contagious disease to obtain healing, but only one had enough gratitude for the new life he'd been given, to come back to offer thanksgiving. As believers, we've all been given new life through Christ and He certainly deserves our gratitude also. Our thanksgiving to God should be a lifestyle and not an occasional phrase we utter, when God gets us out of a jam. He deserves our thanks, not only because of what He does for us but just because He is the all-seeing, all-knowing, and all-powerful God!

So as you think about the goodness of Jesus, His sovereignty, and all He has done for you, "What do you say?"

Today's Devotional Reading: Psalm 100, Luke 17:11-19

Today's Discipline: Begin a daily habit of thanking God for who He is and for what He's done for us. A turkey with all the trimmings is great but we need only a grateful heart to celebrate Thanksgiving every day of the year!

Prayer: Lord God, I thank You for being God alone, for my new life, and for all of the amazing things You do for me. Each day I want to enter into Your gates with Thanksgiving and into Your courts with praise!

Day 17
How Much Do You Weigh?

In our society, asking someone how much they weigh is considered an insult. We protect that information as though it were a social security or credit card number. By contrast, there is a different kind of weight that when kept hidden can cause us trouble in this life and in the next. The weight I am referring to is sin.

In the neighborhood I grew up in, my two brothers and their friends would play touch football in the street. In the winter time, to prevent them from getting sick, all the Mom's would make their son's wear hats, gloves, ear muffs, long underwear, and bulky winter coats. Within minutes of the first snap, every article of clothing intended to keep them warm would be laying in a pile on the curb. Occasionally, there would be one Mom that would holler from the window and threaten to make her son come inside if he didn't put them back on. The common complaint of all the boys was that all those heavy clothes weighed them down. That's exactly what sin does in our lives, it weighs us down and it impedes our ability to serve God.

We don't have to step on a scale to determine the weight of sin in our lives. We need only to examine our behaviors and surrender the ones that separate us from the things of God. Unlike the well-intentioned Mom, there are people in our lives who want us to "put back on" our old ways of thinking, talking, and acting.

We can't be bogged down with the weight of sin. We need focus, agility and endurance in order to run the race of faith. The good news is, as with professional football, we have a stadium full of other saints cheering us on until we reach the goal line!

Today's Devotional Reading: Hebrews 12:1, Romans 6:23, 1 John 1:9

Today's Discipline: Become a Weight Watcher…you don't have to count points but you do have to count the cost!

Prayer: Heavenly Father, there are things in my life that are keeping me from being everything You crafted me to be. You hate sin but not the sinner. Your word says that if I confess my sins, You are faithful and just to forgive me. Help me to shed the weight of sin and to manage my weight by walking with You.

Day 18
Don't Give Up

With the dawning of each New Year, we resolve to change our diets, exercise more, change careers, or make some significant change in our lives, that we deem a much needed and welcomed improvement. No matter how well intentioned, often times we find that as the calendar pages turn, we've gone back to our old eating habits, we've made fewer trips to the gym, and we still have the same resume from three jobs ago.

There are several reasons our goals can go unfulfilled: the demands of work, children, and traumatic events that interrupt our course. Then there is plain old procrastination. We talk about our goals but we can't seem to get started or we start strong and give up just when the going gets tough. Imagine if the traffic light stayed red all the time, we would never get anywhere.

The key to fulfilling our goals is being able to rely on God's strength and not our own. We truly can do all things through Christ who gives us strength! When I do strength training at the gym, and I am in the starting position, my husband who is stronger than I, stands behind me to ensure that I can balance the weight, he lightens the load when it becomes too heavy, and he encourages me to keep going until I make it to the end.

That's what God does for us and more. He gives us strength and He never quits on us! Therefore, we should never quit on ourselves or God. Of course there will be highs and lows but when the dust settles, it's all about making it to the finish line. Why give up when you're almost there? You may be saying, "But I have so far to go!" My response to that is, "If you've started then you're already half-way there!" We must believe that the goals ahead of us are never greater than the God behind us!

Today's Devotional Reading: Philippians 4:13

Today's Discipline: Dust off your goals and dreams and trust that God will give You the strength you need to make them happen.

Prayer: Father God, by myself I am weak but with You there is nothing I cannot accomplish. Help me to follow through on my goals and trust You to make me victorious.

Day 19
Moving Day

When I received confirmation from God to buy my first home, I was so excited that I could not wait to move. After viewing countless homes, I finally walked into the one I knew God had destined for me to own. Within 24 hours my offer was accepted and I was only a few friends and a U-Haul away from moving into my new home. However, there were some details that needed to be taken care of before I could take possession. The same applies when God is about to move us into a new place or level in Him, we must "prepare provisions" to take possession:

1. <u>We must pray to move</u>: I prayed and sought the wisdom of God to reveal to me if, when, where, and how I was going to move. We must also pray and make certain we are moving according to the will of God and not of our own volition.
2. <u>We must be positioned to move</u>: I needed a good credit score to secure my home loan. We must also be

in good standing with God in order to move to higher levels in Him.

3. <u>We must purge to move</u>: I got rid of all the old junk that would have no use in my new home. We must also cleanse and purge our minds of old junk. We cannot take an old mentality into a new dwelling place.
4. <u>We must be packed to move</u>: I packed up all of the necessities and furnishings I would need so they were ready when the movers arrived. When God says, "It's time to move", we should not be running around looking for boxes and bubble wrap.
5. <u>We must maintain our power source</u>: I had to call the electric company to have the power turned on in my home and I had to consistently pay the bill in order to stay connected. We must consistently stay plugged into God to maintain our power on Moving Day and beyond!

Today's Devotional Reading: Joshua 1:10-11

Today's Discipline: When God directs you to take possession of your new place, don't just stand there, bust a move!

Prayer: Dear Lord, I thank You in advance for my new level. As I move in faith, cause me to always prepare provisions for that which You have given me to possess.

Day 20
Mirror, Mirror

Having a healthy self-image is not about having a handsome or pretty face nor does it solely involve having a positive impression of ourselves. A healthy self-image is birthed from learning how to see ourselves the way God sees us. How we see ourselves can directly influence our perception of how others view us.

At God's command, Moses sent men to spy out the land of Canaan. With the exception of two, all of the spies came back with a negative report of what they saw. Although the men agreed the land was fruitful, they did not believe they could contend with the current inhabitants because of their size. They reported, "There we saw giants...and we were like grasshoppers in our own sight, and so we were in their sight." Not only did these spies assessment of the land and its "giants" reflect a poor self-image of themselves but it also echoed a lack of faith in God.

The greatness of others should never cause us to feel small! It's ironic, that these spies likened themselves to grasshoppers. I learned that grasshoppers have "compound eyes," which means the two largest of their five eyes contain thousands of much smaller eyes, which can distort the shape, size, and volume of whatever is in its view. We must not allow who we are in Christ to become distorted by what we see in the mirror or in others.

God told the prophet Samuel, "Do not look at his appearance or at his physical stature...for the Lord does not see as man sees; for man looks at the outward appearance, but the Lord looks at the heart." As we mature in Christ and we look in the mirror, we should see more of God's image staring back at us, than we do our flaws and frailties.

Our worth is never measured by our appearance, abilities, or accomplishments. It is measured by the expensive price Jesus paid to reconcile us back to God.

Today's Devotional Reading: Numbers 13:33, 1 Samuel 16:6-7

Today's Discipline: Check your family tree and discover that your true beauty comes from Our Father's side of the family!

Prayer: Father God, I thank You that I am more than what I look like. I acknowledge that the beauty, power, and light that shines on the outside of me, comes only from You living on the inside of me.

Day 21
The Gift That Keeps On Giving

Ever feel like there is something you're supposed to be doing but you're not sure what it is? Several years ago, I inquisitively asked my brother who is a pastor, "How do I know when I am fulfilling God's purpose for my life?" The answer he gave me was very simple but impactful. He said, "Operate in the gifts God has given you and you will ultimately find yourself walking in the purpose of God." As I gave consideration to the gifts God had given me, I could not see at that time what any of them had to do with God's purpose for me. What took me years to discover is when we use the gifts God gives us in service to others, God will use those same gifts to usher us into His divine purpose.

Take King David for example; before he was anointed as king, he was a skilled musician/harpist. David's gift was the ability to play the harp yet his assignment was to be the king of Israel. Saul, who was king at the time, suffered from a distressing spirit that was only relieved by the beautiful melodies that David played on his harp. What better training for a king to-be, than to be summoned to play private concerts to sooth the depression of the reigning king? David's gift took him from the sheep pasture into the king's palace. Over time, he became the king's armor-bearer, giant slayer, army commander, and eventually the king of Israel.

The bible declares, "A man's gift makes room for him and brings him before great men." This was true in the life of King David and it is true for us today. Who knew that all of the years I spent journaling my thoughts, God would use my gift of writing to mold me into an author? When we use our gifts for service, God can cause them to become transportation to our destination!

Today's Devotional Reading: 1 Samuel 16:14-23, Proverbs 18:16

Today's Discipline: Unwrap your gifts and put them to God's use!

Prayer: Father God, help me to serve others with the gifts You have given me. Lord, I take no credit for my gifts nor do I ever want to take them for granted. Use me for Your good works that I may live with purpose!

Day 22
The Place of God

The pain and sting of abuse, hurt, or betrayal can be difficult to overcome. I believe anything we don't get over is bound to keep us under. Once we are able to recognize that we are in "the place of God," forgiveness is possible.

The story of Joseph and his brothers is a compelling example of forgiveness and restoration. Joseph's brothers sold him into slavery because of jealousy, hate, and fear. Their actions led to Joseph being presumed dead, separated from the love of his father, falsely accused of attempted rape, and sentenced to prison. All of the hell that Joseph went through at the hands of his own brothers, was enough to make anyone want to hate or seek revenge. Years later, when Joseph's brothers learned he was still alive and that he was the only one who could feed them in a time of famine; they feared Joseph would repay their evil deeds with greater evil. The brother's sent a plea of forgiveness to Joseph and his reply was one of faith and spiritual maturity, "Do not be afraid, for am I in the place of God? But as for you, you meant evil against me; _but God_ meant it for good." The key words of Joseph's response are "but God."

God did not orchestrate the misery that Joseph went through, however the sin of his brothers was the cause. Yet God used those offenses to affect His will which was to bring about a far greater destiny for Joseph. As a result, Joseph was able to see the providence of God in all that he endured and was able to help his family despite what they did to him.

Forgiveness does not mean that we excuse the offense; it means we reclaim our power from the offender.

Today's Devotional Reading: Genesis 50:15-21, Mark 11:26

Today's Discipline: Start by making a list of those you need to forgive and begin to pray for them.

Prayer: Father God, help me to forgive those who have hurt me or wronged me. I recognize the only way I can be free of the offense, is to forgive the offender. I don't want anything to stand in the way of Your forgiveness of my sins or the good You have planned for my life.

Day 23
The Good Wife

Contrary to the popular portrayals of wives on television today, a good wife is not a docile wife of a politician who smiles and "stands by her man," as he admits to the world his extramarital affairs; neither is she a woman who garners the title "housewife" without the covenant or commitment of marriage. There is something very special about being a wife. The bible says, "He who finds a wife finds a good thing and obtains favor from the Lord." Note that the bible does not say that a man who gets married finds a good thing.

Several years ago, I prayed to God about getting married. God's immediate response to me was, "Are you a wife?" Obviously, God already knew the answer to that question and soon after, I came to realize also that I was not ready to be a wife. God showed me through scripture that marriage is a spiritual covenant that requires spiritual attributes. Like many women, I had a desire to be married but I did not possess the spiritual tools to be a wife. This revelation re-shaped my prayer about marriage and began my quest to discover what it truly means to be a wife.

God revealed to me that a wife is called to be a cover and not a wet blanket. The covering of a wife provides refuge, relationship, and respect, which are three primary needs of a man. A wife (being created from the rib of man) covers not only the heart of her husband but his entire being, while a wet blanket exposes the vulnerable parts of her husband for all to see. A wife covers her husband in prayer and ignites his spirit, while a wet blanket extinguishes his fire and douses his dreams.

A good wife understands that God is her first love and her true bridegroom. A good wife is whole and complete in Christ. A good wife is a good wife long before she says, "I Do!"

Today's Devotional Reading: Proverbs 18:22, Proverbs 19:14, Proverbs 31

Today's Discipline: Reconsider your definition of a wife or a husband and ask God to equip you where you may be lacking.

Prayer: Lord, whether I am married or single, teach me how to be a good wife or husband. A wedding is but for a day, a spouse is for a lifetime.

Day 24
Father Knows Best

A friend asked me, "If everything happens according to God's will, what is the point of praying?" That is a question many of us have asked at some point in our prayer life. When we pray, we expect God to do that which we ask of Him. The difficult part is accepting that what we ask of Him may not be "according to His will."

When my cousin and dear friend, Shermaine Nikki Harrison was diagnosed with breast cancer in 1999, it never occurred to me that she may not survive. Many people began to petition God for her healing. In fact, an annual prayer breakfast was established to raise awareness and to offer prayer and resources for Nikki and others who were impacted by the disease. God's will for Nikki was to endure breast cancer with courage, laughter, and faithfulness. With divine grace that is exactly what she accomplished! Her faith encouraged others to never give up hope in what seems like a hopeless situation. On September 3, 2003, after years of prayers and treatment, Nikki went home to be with the Lord. She was a rare and radiant light that illuminated most brightly in the face of adversity and trials.

Jesus, acknowledged to God that "all things are possible for You," as He prayed to God for an alternative to death on the cross. But by faith He was able to say "nevertheless, not what I will but what You will." What I have come to understand is that the purpose of prayer is not to change God's will or His mind. Prayer helps to change our minds and our perspective of God's will. We must be confident that our prayers are never fruitless or in vain. God invites us to pray, therefore it can never be unproductive. Prayer strengthens our relationship with God and helps us to trust that Our Father truly does know best.

Today's Devotional Reading: 1 John 5:14, Philippians 4:6-7, Mark 14:36

Today's Discipline: Begin a prayer journal and record how God answers your prayers. This can offer insight into the will of God and it will reassure you that He hears you when you pray.

Prayer: Father God, I want to be obedient to Your desires more than my own. Help me to always surrender to Your will and to trust that You always know what is best. Lord, show me how to pray according to Your will and grant me the peace to accept your response.

Day 25
The G.O.A.T.

In the sport of boxing, the answer to the question "Who is the G.O.A.T.?" (The Greatest of All Time) is often argued. Depending on the enthusiast you survey, the answer will vary from Joe Louis to Rocky Marciano, or from Muhammad Ali to Mike Tyson. The lists of these boxing greats go on and on. When it comes to the true, undisputed, greatest heavyweight of all time, my answer is simply...Jesus Christ!

Let's look at the tale of the tape. He hails from Bethlehem by way of the beginning of time. His truth (the bible) continues to be the world's best seller and is translated in over 2,000 languages. He is undefeated and incapable of losing a fight. His reach is beyond measure and nothing or no one is a match for His righteous right hand. He is the only heavyweight that can assure us a fixed fight and make death take a dive. He requires no trainer or cut man in His corner. He has the shortest nickname in fight history, "I AM," but His robe reads, "King of Kings and Lord of Lords!" He doesn't wear a belt around His waist but He wears many crowns on His head. Sin and death were His toughest opponents and even they were KO'd, and there will be no rematch! Jesus cannot be disqualified, knocked down, or knocked out.

Ali may have floated like a butterfly and stung like a bee but only Jesus Christ can say to death, "Where is your sting? O Hades, where is your victory?" Jesus guarantees all believers victory over sin and death after giving them both a final knockout punch! Don't call it a comeback, He's been the G.O.A.T. forever!

Today's Devotional Reading: 1 Corinthians 15:50-57, Revelation 19:11-16

Today's Discipline: Meditate on the scripture readings and remember that we can never lose when we allow God to fight our battles.

Prayer: Father God, I acknowledge Your Sovereignty and Power in all the world. Thank You for giving me the victory over sin and death. Of all of the battle's You've fought on my behalf, this one guarantees I will spend eternity with You. Thank You for conquering everything that would try to separate me from You.

Day 26
Are You Certain?

In modern medicine, there is a diagnosis and treatment for nearly every ailment. Interestingly, when you give consideration to the prescription drug advertisements on television, the list of side effects announced at the end of the ad are usually more severe than the actual ailment being treated. I imagine the condition of the woman in today's lesson was complicated by the side effects of the various treatments she endured. This woman had a condition of persistent bleeding for twelve years. The bible says she "suffered many things from many physicians. She had spent all that she had and was no better, but rather grew worse."

As I meditated on today's reading, I became intrigued at how Mark's gospel describes this woman. He says, "Now a <u>certain</u> woman had a flow of blood for twelve years." It is likely that Mark used the term "certain" to indicate that the woman was not named or particularly specified. But I'd like to suggest he used the term "certain" to indicate that this woman was free of doubt, destined, and sure. How do I know this? Her actions suggested that she was "certain":

1.) When the woman heard about Jesus, she was <u>certain</u> that she had to get into His presence. (vs. 27)

2.) She was <u>certain</u> that if she could just touch the garment of Jesus she would be healed of her affliction. (vs. 28)

3.) She was <u>certain</u> that she felt the manifestation of healing taking place in her body. (vs. 29)

With one touch, this certain woman was taken from condition to position. Jesus restored her physically, renewed her financially, re-established her socially, and reconciled her to Him as His daughter…all because she was <u>CERTAIN</u>! In like manner, we must believe that if He did it for this certain woman, He can <u>certainly</u> do the same for us!

Today's Devotional Reading: Mark 5: 25-34, Ephesians 3:20

Today's Discipline: Do whatever it takes to get into the presence of Jesus!

Prayer: Lord, when I am faced with physical affliction and illness, I will call upon Your name, Jehovah Rapha (The God Who Heals). Your word declares that You are "able to do exceedingly abundantly above all that we ask or think, according to the power that works in us."

Day 27
No Laughing Matter

Have you ever heard the saying, "If you want to make God laugh tell Him your plans?" Well, one day Sarah overheard God's plan for her to bear a child in old age and Sarah laughed. In fact, she "laughed within herself" saying, "An old woman like me? Get pregnant? With this old man of a husband?" Genesis 18:12 ("MSG") Sarah believed that the time on her proverbial biological clock had expired and there was no way she at 90 years old and her centenarian husband would ever bear children. After questioning Sarah's sarcastic and faithless response, God countered and asked "Is anything too hard for the Lord?" What a powerful statement! When things are humanly impossible that's when God shows Himself most strong and powerful. Abraham was 100 years old and Sarah was 90 when she bore their first child Isaac whose name ironically means "laughter."

A common mistake we often make is placing limits on what God can do based upon our own limited thinking.

There is our time and then there's "the appointed time" and rarely do they run on the same schedule. In 1992, after having both of my hips replaced, it became increasingly difficult to get in and out of my car. I prayed to God about purchasing something more comfortable but the car I wanted was out of my price range. Shortly after, I was entered into a raffle sponsored by a local radio station and the grand prize was a brand new SUV. Three days prior to the drawing God revealed to me in a dream that the new truck was mine and I believed Him! I told friends, family, and co-workers and like Sarah, many of them laughed in disbelief at the mere thought that I would win a brand new truck. Not only did God deliver on His promise, but that truck was far greater than the car I prayed about. The icing on the cake was I was able to drive it for 13 years without a single car note!

Through this experience and many others I have learned to believe that there is nothing too hard for God! He can bring forth life in every barren area of our lives when we trust Him and in the end He always gets the last laugh.

Today's Devotional Reading: Genesis 18:9-15, Genesis 21:1-3

Today's Discipline: Reinforce todays reading with Jeremiah 32:26-27 and remember that when we doubt God's power...the joke is always on us!

Prayer: Lord God, I believe that there is nothing too hard for You. May my laughter always come from a place of joy and anticipation of Your power manifested and never from a place of disbelief.

Day 28
Don't Look Back

For most of us, our past has lots of good memories and fun times, but they are also checkered with mistakes, failures, and even poor reputations. There is definitely no harm in reminiscing on the good in our past. The danger is when we dwell on the negative things from our past. Someone once told me the one thing we can never have is a better past. Looking back can be very tempting, especially when we don't find ourselves where we desire to be, or when we fear where we are going. Often times we have a tendency to gravitate to what is familiar, comfortable, and safe; but when we're not willing to step out on faith to explore the new things God has for us, chaos and dysfunction can appear familiar, comfortable, and safe.

The apostle Paul was a great teacher on how to keep our past in perspective. Paul would be the first to admit that he didn't have it all together. In fact, he said, "The one thing I do, forgetting those things which are behind and reaching forward to those things which are ahead, I press toward the goal for the prize of the upward call of God in Christ Jesus." Paul understood that this life is like a track meet. We can't run our race while constantly looking back, for when we do we lose momentum. The more we look back the more we'll see our past gaining on us. We must stay in our lane, run our race with endurance, all while keeping our eyes on the prize.

Our past is not an old friend that requires checking in on or keeping in touch with, however, we don't need to attempt to erase it entirely from our memory either. "Forgetting those things which are behind" means to redirect our focus and our energy on what is ahead. God put our eyes on the front of our face and not on the back of our head for a reason. Looking back is like driving a car using only your rear view mirror, the only place it gets us is in a jam!

Today's Devotional Reading: Philippians 3:13-14

Today's Discipline: Focus on your present; that is why it is called a gift.

Prayer: Father God, there are many things in my past that I am not proud of and You know them all and You love me just the same. The good news is when I know better I can do better. Help me to always keep what's ahead in my view.

Day 29
Lemon Pound Cake

One of my favorite pastimes is baking and one of my favorite deserts is lemon pound cake. Aside from the fact that lemon pound cake tastes out of this world, its ingredients symbolize the good and bad of life. Let me share with you the ingredients to my simple recipe:

*<u>Eggs</u>: we must be cracked in order to get to the sunny side.

*<u>Baking Powder</u>: helps us rise to the occasion when we fall flat.

*<u>Lemon Zest</u>: the strength of our beautiful fragrance is only revealed when our skin is broken.

*<u>Butter</u>: gets rid of our lumps and helps us to become smooth.

*<u>Salt</u>: makes what life dishes out more palatable.

*<u>Flour</u>: keeps us from falling apart.

*<u>Sugar</u>: makes us sweet.

*<u>Vanilla</u>: enhances the flavors of all the other ingredients.

Some of these ingredients if eaten separately will leave us feeling sick and wanting to throw in the towel. But when you mix them all together the result is always good and worth the wait! The bible declares in Romans 8:28, "and we know that ALL THINGS WORK TOGETHER FOR GOOD to those who love God, to those who are called according to His purpose."

In life, there will be days when we are pinched, sifted, cracked, beaten and grated. There will also be days when life is so sweet we should have a mouth full of cavities. The thing to remember is that God takes the bitter and the sweet moments of our lives, blends them all together, and creates something magnificent!

Today's Devotional Reading: Romans 8:24-39

Today's Discipline: Spend time reflecting on how God has used the bad times of your life for your good and then begin to praise Him!

Prayer: Lord God, You always know what is best for me and You know what is required to bring out Your best in me. Sometimes it may not feel good but I trust that it is for my good. Help me to see You in everything I go through, for I know if I can see You I am not alone.

Day 30
This Is A Stick Up!

Growing up in a single parent household there were times when our Mom would let her 5 children eat dinner before she ate dinner. Being the baby, I thought it was because she wasn't hungry but as I grew older I learned that she would allow us to eat her portion so we would not be hungry. Before long, God blessed our pantry in such a way that our Mom could set aside for herself a portion of every meal knowing that there was more than enough for her children to eat.

One time our Mom purchased some premium pecans that she planned to use to bake a special dessert but someone in the family decided to over indulge by secretly consuming the entire bag of pecans. Needless to say we were all punished and the identity of the pecan bandit remains a mystery to this day. These childhood memories remind me of today's scripture reading Malachi 3:8, "Will a man rob

God? Yet you have robbed Me! But you say in what way have we robbed You? In tithes and offering."

Similarly, as our Mom set aside a portion of the abundance for herself, God has the right to require that we set aside a portion of His abundance for Him. The difference is God's portion doesn't sustain Him, it sustains us! We wrongfully believe that the 90% portion that we keep for ourselves is what sustains us, but really it's the 10% tithe that we trust back to God by faith that sustains us.

Think about it, all that we have already belongs to God. Our money, our talents, our time, our praise...they ALL belong to God. When we withhold or rob Him of these things we are essentially sticking up God's portion. God doesn't need anything from us. We give to God as an acknowledgement that He is the Supplier of all our needs and we trust Him to perpetually replenish our resources. Even in the Garden of Eden, Adam and Eve ate of the one tree that God set aside for Himself and it changed the course of history and introduced sin into the world.

Today's Devotional Reading: Malachi 3: 8, Genesis 2:16-17

Today's Discipline: Examine any area of your life where you may be withholding from God. Remember, a hand can only receive when there is nothing in it!

Prayer: Father, forgive me for robbing You, for I now know that if I surrender everything to You, I will want for nothing!

Day 31
It's Only a Test

Have you ever been engrossed in a television program and all of a sudden you're startled by a deafening sound from the emergency broadcast system? This system is commonly used for severe local weather alerts, much like the weather Peter experienced in today's passage of scripture. When the system is activated, it produces a sound called the "attention signal," hence the repulsive noise. During activation, a repeating banner displays on your television screen which reads, "This Is Only a Test!"

In similar fashion, most of the turbulence and storms we encounter in life are merely God's "attention signal" indicating that "this is only a test." God desires for us to keep our attention on Him especially during our most dire situations. When we begin to focus more on our circumstances and we fail to see Jesus in the midst of it all, like Peter, we may begin to sink. Interestingly, earlier in this passage (verses 22-24), we see that the wind was boisterous and the waves of the sea were tossed while Peter was in the boat. Many times our condition hasn't changed but our outlook has. Usually, this is a good thing but not in Peter's case. Do you know we are safer out of the boat walking with Jesus than we are in the boat waiting for the storm to pass?

Peter was among the other disciples who had just witnessed Jesus heal the sick and feed a multitude of 5,000 people. In fact, immediately following this fish feast, Jesus commanded the disciples to get into the boat to go before Him to their next destination. It was there that Peter's faith would be tested. This demonstrates to us that often times when we've just had a mountain-top experience, immediately following, we may be tested in the valley.

Although Peter briefly began to sink, the fact remains that Peter did walk on water. So the next time you find yourself in the midst of a storm, remind yourself that this is only a test and when you respond with faith, you'll pass with flying colors!

Today's Devotional Reading: Matthew 14:25-33, 2 Corinthians 5:7

Today's Discipline: In the midst of your storms, pray to God for an "out of the boat" experience and trust Him to make the water your pavement.

Prayer: Lord God, thank You that the storms of life come only to elevate my faith. Grant me the courage to be a water-walker and the wisdom to know that with You sinking is not an option.

Day 32
You Are Forgiven...Kind Of

Have you ever extended forgiveness to someone and then continued to behave uncivilized toward them? Or maybe you've said, "I forgive you," but then you exiled the person from your life? Forgiveness is often a difficult task for many of us, but it is required of us as believers if we desire for God to forgive us of our offenses. Often times our approach to forgiveness is with the intent of never having to deal with the person who hurt us again. But what if God said to us, "I forgive you but I don't want to see, talk, or deal with you ever again?"

There may be times when forgiveness may not lead to reconciliation but I believe it is the desire of God that we work toward living peaceably with those we have forgiven. The bible offers many illustrations where people were not only forgiven but they were restored and reconciled back to those they harmed.

Take for instance Joseph, who was sold into slavery by his brothers and presumed dead by all who knew him. Not only did Joseph forgive his brothers but he said, "You shall be near to me, you and your children." Or like the prodigal son who defiantly left home thinking the grass would be greener on the other side. He squandered all of his inheritance because he thought he knew what was best for him more than his father. In like manner, we often behave like we know more than our Heavenly Father.

The best illustration in the bible of forgiveness involves you and me. Jesus became the ultimate sacrifice for our sins. He died on a cross for crimes He did not commit. Jesus did all of this so we could be forgiven of our sins, restored, and reconciled back to God. When we're faced with a situation where we are in need of forgiveness, or when it is necessary that we forgive someone else, it may help to remember all that Jesus did so that we could be forgiven and be in right standing with God.

Today's Devotional Reading: Genesis 45:4-10, Luke 15:11-32

Today's Discipline: Ask God for help with forgiving those who have hurt you and for the wisdom to determine if restoration is His will.

Prayer: Dear Heavenly Father, help me to not only say the words "I forgive you," but give me the strength to receive those I've forgiven back into my life according to Your will. Thank You Father for not cutting me off from a relationship with You all the times when I've broken Your heart.

Day 33
Charge It!

While in a Christian bookstore, I ran into a family friend who shared that she was looking for a book about "Power." She was dealing with some issues and felt they were happening in part because she had lost her spiritual power. She also mentioned that she had not been praying and seeking the Lord's guidance as she regularly does. I carefully reminded her that if she believes she lost her power then at some point she was in possession of her power. I suggested rather than search for a book about Power, she should consider plugging back into her Power Source.

Ironically, earlier that day, I noticed my cell phone which I had completely charged 3 days prior, now had a battery life of 20%. I had not made one call or text but the phones power charge was nearly depleted within 72 hours. The only thing I could do was plug it back into the power source for a recharge.

This is exactly what happens when Christians disconnect from God. We can be completely charged up on Sunday but by Tuesday our power has already begun to diminish. I shared this experience with my friend in the bookstore as a reminder that no matter how charged up we think we are from a good Sunday service; if we don't stay connected to our Power Source daily through prayer, bible study, worship, and giving, our power will surely begin to deplete.

Often times our disconnection from God is not intentional. Life has a way of bringing more responsibilities and obligations our way and before we know it our spiritual battery life is dead.

Jesus said, *"I am the vine, you are the branches. He who abides in Me, and I in him, bears much fruit; for without Me you can do nothing."* Church services, just like the lithium ion batteries in our cell phones emit a lot of power, but neither is designed to hold a charge for more than a few days. We must be intentional with staying charged up!

Today's Devotional Reading: John 15:4-5

Today's Discipline: Take inventory of your power source and make sure you are fully charged at all times!

Prayer: Father God, I am grateful today that You are the stem that causes me to blossom. I realize Lord that the moment I allow myself to become separated from You, I will begin to wither. Impart in me new ways to stay rooted in You.

Day 34
Closer than You Think

One of my precious Sunday school children eagerly raised his hand to answer my question, "Where is God?" As soon as I called his name he quickly retorted that God is far away in Heaven. He emphatically shared that even though God is far away, we can talk to Him by praying. I explained to the children that although God lives in Heaven, He also is in the earth and in our hearts, and everywhere all at the same time. It occurred to me that my student's impression of the distance of God's habitation was not unlike our impression at times. There are moments in life when we also feel like God is far away.

One morning while sitting in rush hour traffic I was feeling a little spiritually disjointed. With plenty of time on my hands, I decided to pray. As I slowly inched along among the sea of cars going nowhere, I noticed the safety warning inscribed in the side view mirrors on my truck. The words read, "Objects in mirror are closer than they appear." It's interesting how you can see something every day and never really pay attention to its beauty or meaning. That particular morning, my side view mirror ministered to me by reminding me that God was closer to me and my situation than it seemed. Contrary to popular belief, perception is not always reality! The side view mirror has a convex or arched design to help increase our field of view. The drawback to this design is that everything in the mirror appears smaller and much further away than it really is.

Fortunately for us, we serve a gigantic God who is bigger than all of our problems and is as near to us as the air we breathe. "Am I a God near at hand," says the Lord, and not a God afar off?" God makes it lovingly clear in His word that He "will never leave you nor forsake you."

Today's Devotional Reading: Jeremiah 23:23-24, Hebrews 13:5

Today's Discipline: Whatever you're going through, whatever trial you may be facing, make sure your field of view has a constant reminder that God Is Closer than You Think!

Prayer: Father God, when life gets me down and situations seem hard to bear, help me Lord to remember that You are always near. Lord, I welcome Your presence in every area of my life.

Day 35

Membership Has Its Privileges

It is not by happenstance that the Bible reminds us to "forget not all His benefits." If we're not careful, life's challenges can cause us to FORGET that as blood bought believers, we are entitled to certain privileges! Take a moment to think about what this truly means. The scripture declares in Psalm 103 that the benefits of God are forgiveness, healing, deliverance, love, mercy and much more! As we see in this passage, there are so many benefits in being a child of the Most High God. But the only way to truly walk in the complete knowledge of who we are in Christ is to meditate on His word day and night. We must research our lineage so we may obtain our full birthright and all of the "perks" that come along with our holy heritage.

Speaking of perks, in a world where everything costs, we are constantly looking for ways to save or get more bang for our buck. Retailers are in heated competition to prove to the consumer that there are enormous benefits to joining their particular savings club. We proudly exhibit our club cards on our key rings which display more membership advantages than keys to our homes and cars. We have our bonus cards, our gas rewards, our frequent flyer points, our senior discounts, and don't forget our frozen yogurt punch cards.

But have we forgotten about the greatest benefits of all? With God's membership rewards program there are no forms to fill out or key rings to carry. There are no email floods or coupons to print. All that is required is that we say "Yes" to His will. Membership is free in the family of Christ and the amount you are saved is always 100%. Let's take a moment to reflect on our "spiritual savings." How many times has the Lord saved us from sin, sickness, foreclosure, abuse, debt, abandonment, low self-esteem, and the consequences of our own choices? The list goes on and on.

Just as we are faithful to the vendors who give us ten cents off for every fifty dollars we spend, we must be even more faithful to our God who paid our debt in full and sought nothing in return. Remember...the savings we yield from God's membership rewards program reaps an eternal gain that no man, grocery chain, or drugstore could ever give.

Today's Devotional Reading: Psalm 103:2-3

Today's Discipline: Meditate on today's scripture reading and celebrate that with God's benefits, you are fully covered and there are no co-pays or deductibles!

Prayer: Father God, thank You that Your benefits never expire. I am eternally grateful to be covered by Your richest blessings. With all that is within me, I bless Your holy name!

Day 36
Son-roof

In my childhood community of Washington Square, there was a pavilion that sat upon a hill next to the basketball court. All of the kids referred to it as "the sunroof." We called it the sunroof because whenever it was extremely hot, the roof of the pavilion protected us from the heat and offered shelter from the rain. Many times a summer storm would quickly form and there would be no time to run all the way home. The sunroof provided quick refuge from heavy downpours, thunder, lightning, and sweltering heat. Even meteorologists warn that when a storm is approaching we should be prepared to find shelter immediately, preferably a pre-designated location.

Sometimes we find ourselves seeking immediate shelter from life's heavy downpours and the sweltering heat of Satan's fiery darts. Fortunately for us, Psalm 27:5 declares, "For in the time of trouble He shall hide me in His pavilion; in the secret place of His tabernacle. He shall hide me; He shall set me high upon a rock." Just as we should have a plan in place when natural storms and heatwaves occur, we need to have a designated place of refuge when spiritual storms occur.

The Son of God is our "Son-roof" and our refuge in the time of trouble. Proverbs 18:10 confirms, "the name of the Lord is a strong tower; the righteous run to it and are safe." There is no greater name than Jesus. Put Your trust in Him and He will always keep a roof over your head!

Today's Devotional Reading: Psalm 27:5, Proverbs 18:10

Today's Discipline: Examine the structure and safety of your shelter by making sure your foundation is in Christ.

Prayer: Lord God, there is nothing like the peace of Your protection. I am grateful that whenever I am in need of covering, You are always there to shield me from all harm and danger.

Day 37
Come Out With Your Hands Up!

The call of God on our lives can sometimes be an intimidating and frightening feat. Our natural minds may begin to think we won't be able to do that which God has called us to do. We begin to think "I'm not qualified," "Who would listen to me?" or "It's too much responsibility." Much like Saul, when he was told by the prophet Samuel that God had appointed him to be the king of Israel. Saul's first instinct was to go into hiding, more specifically he hid among the baggage. Saul was quick to point out to Samuel that he was from the least of the tribes of Israel. Sometimes it is easy for us to refer back to the things that make us feel small when God has called us to do something huge!

The people of Israel demanded a king to judge them and had rejected God as their King. This brings to mind the soul stirring group, The O'Jays hit song called "Give the People What They Want." God did just that, He gave the people exactly what they wanted, a king, by way of Saul. Saul would ultimately prove to God and the people what God already knew, which was Saul was not truly God's choice. But the fact remains Saul was called by God.

When God calls us and anoints us for a specific work, it's like He is issuing a spiritual warrant for our arrest. As in the natural, a spiritual warrant does not always lead to an immediate arrest. Many like Saul, go into hiding and some remain on the run for years. God doesn't want to put an All-Points Bulletin out on us to bring us into His custody. He wants us to respond in obedience the moment He gives the assignment. He desires that we freely turn ourselves in to His authority and surrender to His will and call on our lives.

God will always be in pursuit of those He has called, the question is… will you come out with your hands up?

Today's Devotional Reading: 1 Samuel 10:21-23

Today's Discipline: Make a to-do list of all the things that God is calling You to do and with outstretched hands, surrender to His will for your life.

Prayer: Father God, I desire to do all You have called me to do. Crucify any fear within me that may be causing me to run from Your will for my life. Lord, I acknowledge that being in Your custody is never bondage, rather it is true liberty and freedom!

Day 38

In God We Trust

One of the most prevalent issues in this life for Christians and non-Christians is the issue of self-worth. Sometimes our negative experiences can cause us to feel unworthy.

Whenever I minister to women at various speaking engagements, the subject of self-worth and value almost always is a concern. One of the tools I use to demonstrate worth is a $20 dollar bill. I start out with a crisp $20 dollar bill with no flaws. Then I take the money and crumble it up into a tiny ball, I drop it on the floor, and step on it. Sometimes I even rip a small tear on it. I then unravel the bill and ask the question, "How much is it worth?" I do this to demonstrate that no matter how much we are torn, dropped, stepped on, or mistreated, it doesn't change our value.

Typically, we determine the value of something based on how much it cost. When an insurance company appraises a home, jewelry, or car, they assess the current and future worth of these assets. They also assess what similar assets are being sold for and their replacement value. In other words...what's it worth??? The worth of something in terms of its monetary value is often determined by the value of another item for which it can be exchanged. Jesus appraised the value of the woman in today's reading as priceless with a single word...DAUGHTER! When He called her Daughter, He reconciled her into the family of Christ. Her value is priceless because it cost Jesus EVERYTHING (HIS VERY LIFE) that she may be a child of God! We will always know our value when we remember how much it costs Jesus to purchase us with His precious blood! Hallelujah!

Just like the tattered $20 dollar bill, our worth does not depreciate as we go through tough times; and also like the $20 dollar bill, no matter what we go through, we can still say, "In God We Trust!"

Today's Devotional Reading: Mark 5:34, Romans 5:8

Today's Discipline: Try the $20 dollar bill demonstration and re-discover your worth!

Prayer: Father God, because of Your love for me, I have been fully and forever redeemed! Help me to be confident that I am worth everything to You and to trust that You regard me as priceless!

Day 39
It's Not for Show!

There was a time in my life when I would use my gifts as a means to validate myself in the eyes of others, rather than honoring God with the gift He gave me by using it to serve others. Sadly, I would feel a sense of validation at the mere thought of someone discovering that I had a God given ability or talent. Although I was not using the gift, just having it gave me a false sense of accomplishment. Much like a millionaire with a garage full of expensive cars. Rarely are the cars driven, but sometimes allowing others a quick gawk of their prized possessions is more gratifying than using it to give a ride to someone in need.

How is it that I was more comfortable with others noticing I had potential than actually working toward realizing my potential? Where did this standard of marginality come from? When I was in the ninth grade I participated in the cheerleading "tryouts" in my junior high school. I should say I went "out" but I certainly did not "try." I went to the audition resting on my reputation as a great cheerleader and co-captain of the rival school from which I had transferred. I approached it as though I could transfer my previous distinction as a varsity cheerleader into a new position that I was not willing to earn. Imagine my surprise when the new squad list was posted and my name was not on it. I quickly realized that no one cared about how good I used to be. They wanted to see the excellence in me now!

Needless to say, that experience was a huge blow to my ego, not to mention a very valuable lesson that I still have to draw from every now and then.

While in prison, the apostle Paul wrote a letter to Timothy encouraging him, "to stir up the gift of God which is in you." We must be careful that we do not allow our gifts to lay dormant or take them for granted by using them for our glory instead of God's. We must continue to fan the flame of our gifts so that we don't lose our spiritual fire for serving God and others!

Today's Devotional Reading: 2 Timothy 1:6

Today's Discipline: Are your gifts and talents simmering on the back burner? If so, turn up the heat, stir them up, and pour them out that others may be edified and God may be glorified!

Prayer: Father God, thank You for every gift and talent You have produced in me. Lord, please forgive me for every time I've used my gifts with selfish motives.

Day 40
Spiritual Withholdings

Ever since I can remember, Christmas has always been my favorite holiday. Growing up, our house was filled with love, laughter, faith, family, and friends...especially at Christmas. Although money was not in abundance, it never stopped me and my siblings from draping the Toys R Us wish book across our laps and shouting, "I want that!" with competing index fingers. One Christmas in particular, my oldest brother wanted a motorized box car. Needless to say, like many children, our parents did not get us every item we put on our Christmas lists. Not because we were on the proverbial "naughty list" and not because of limited resources. Some of the things we asked for simply were not good for us.

As adults, we are no longer waiting with hopeful anticipation for Hot Wheel Race Tracks or Barbie's Dream House but there are jobs and dreams that we desire to see fulfilled and we find ourselves asking, "When Lord?" Have you ever had the feeling that God is holding out on you? You work hard for something, you pray for it and you still don't get what you want?

The word of God tells us, "No good thing will He withhold from those who walk uprightly." Which means if God is withholding anything from us than it cannot be good for us. It doesn't necessarily mean that it is not God's will for it to happen. It simply means it may not be our season or we may not be equipped to handle the responsibility or the pitfalls that comes with our request.

For example, one of my favorite treats is Hershey's Chocolate Kisses and I discovered that our childhood dog Princess had a hankering for them also. So I counted them out in twos, "One for me and one for you...one for me and one for you." As I innocently shared my chocolates with Princess she made no objections. I quickly learned at her expense that chocolate is toxic when consumed by dogs. Thankfully, things turned out okay for Princess but after her chocolate scare, the sight of shiny foil was enough for her to run for the hills.

Our dreams and desires may not make us sick, but when given to us before we are ready for them, they can spell big trouble for us in ways we are unable to forecast. Thank God that He can see the end from the beginning and know when to put a hold on our spiritual bank accounts.

Today's Devotional Reading: Psalm 84:11

Today's Discipline: Give God praise for the withholdings He has placed on your spiritual bank account and thank Him that your account is not overdrawn!

Prayer: Father God, I confess that I may not always see beyond my wants and desires. Thank You Lord for withholding the things that are not good for my life at this time.

Final Thoughts

Throughout my life, God has blessed me with so many wonderful people who have helped to till my soil, plant good seeds, and water me with love, that I may reap the harvest of Joy. In particular, Mr. Earl Waters, a family friend and member of my childhood church was one of those people. He was one on a short list of people that addressed me by my middle name, Joy. When I was twenty five years old, he gave me a gift that I will cherish for the rest of my life. Mr. Earl shared with me that I was blessed with a middle name that would serve as a daily reminder of how God desires for me to live my life. He said, "True Joy comes when you serve Jesus first, then others, and then yourself." Mr. Earl has since gone on to be with The Lord, but his words of wisdom are engraved on the tablets of my heart.

Thank you all for partnering with me on this journey of faith. May God continue to enlighten the eyes of your understanding, pour out His richest blessings over your life, and give to you THE OIL OF JOY!

Blessings,

Nicole Joy Holmes

Topical Index

Being A Child of God	Day 10
Being Like God	Day 13
Call of God	Day 37
Connecting With God	Day 9
Desires	Day 40
Easter/Resurrection Sunday	Day 4
Encouragement	Day 18
Faith	Day 26
Forgiveness	Day 22
Forgiveness	Day 32
Friendship	Day 12
Giving	Day 30
God's Benefits	Day 35
God's Love	Day 2
God's Presence	Day 34
God's Promises	Day 27
Grief	Day 15
Guidance	Day 14
Letting Go	Day 6
Marriage	Day 23
Negative Thoughts	Day 8
Power	Day 33
Prayer	Day 24

Preparation .... Day 19
Purpose .... Day 21
Recipe of Life .... Day 29
Safety .... Day 5
Self-Image .... Day 20
Self-Worth .... Day 38
Protection... Day 36
Sin .... Day 17
Sovereignty of God .... Day 25
Spiritual Birth .... Day 1
Spiritual Gifts .... Day 39
Spiritual Nourishment .... Day 11
Tests .... Day 31
Thanksgiving .... Day 16
The Past .... Day 28
Waiting on God .... Day 7
Worry .... Day 3

Made in the USA
Middletown, DE
31 July 2015